The Snake in the C

Part 6: The White Car

The focus in this book is on the split digraphs

'a-e, i-e, o-e' in the words:

lane   snake   cave   place   trace

flames   made   make   white   side

time   closer   home   woke   stone

Wellington woke up. He was in the kennel. The snake? The tunnel? The dragon? Were they real or were they just a dream?

1

He wanted to go to the cave to look for the tunnel, the dragon and the snake. Lotty and Kevin wanted to go with him.

Wellington let the little dogs go down the lane with him. When they reached the rocks, he told them not to go inside the cave.

Wellington went into the cave by himself. He
looked for the ledge. He found it. There was no
snake on it.

He looked for the tunnel in the side of the cave.

He could not find it. A large stone was in its

place. It was too big to move.

He looked for the big snake behind all the rocks.

He could not find any trace of it. He thought he

must have made it up in his dream.

If he did make it up, then the snake was not real. He did not have to worry about it. It was time to go home.

On his way out of the cave he saw something white on the floor. He went closer to look at it. It was a white candle.

Oh no! He had a white candle in his dream. He lit the dragon's flames with a white candle. Oh no! What was real? What was a dream?

Wellington ran out of the cave. He ran past

Kevin and Lotty and across the field. 'Oh no!

What has scared him now?' they wondered.

Vowel graphemes used in this book

ay, a-e:	snake cave lane made make way flames trace place
ea, ie:	real dream reached field
y, i, i-e:	by inside side find behind time white
o, o-e:	woke told stone home closer
oo:	too
oo:	look looked
ow, ou:	down out about found now
or:	for floor or
er:	closer wondered
ar:	large
are:	scared

LITTLE HISTORIES

Greek
Times

Christopher Maynard

Kingfisher

Contents

In the beginning...

Just under 3,000 years ago, a number of small Greek cities began to grow in size and power. The people who lived in the cities made marvellous buildings and created beautiful works of art. They developed new ideas about art, science and government, and little by little their ideas spread – at first to Mediterranean countries, and then beyond.

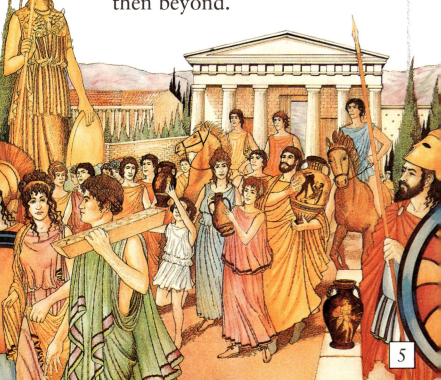

A land of cities

G reece is very mountainous. Its
cities were like small countries or
states, cut off from their neighbours by
rugged mountain ranges.

Troy

Mount
Olympos

Athens

Olympia

Sparta

Mediterranean Sea

Crete

In earliest times, each city was ruled by a king, or one or more powerful men. Later, in some cities, all the freemen shared in running the government. This is called democracy. The Greeks were the first people to practise it.

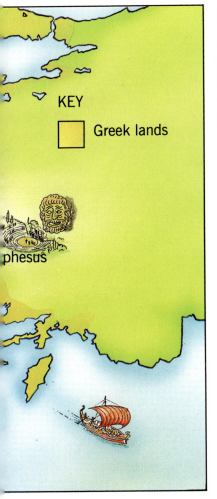

KEY

Greek lands

phesus

Greece

▽ Alexander the Great and his father, King Philip of Macedon, were the first people to try to rule over all the Greek city-states, about 2,300 years ago.

Going to war

Fighting often broke out between the city-states. The most powerful ones, Athens and Sparta, went to war many times. The Spartans had a full-time army, but the other cities only called their freemen to arms when a war started.

Greek foot soldiers were called hoplites. They fought shoulder to shoulder, in closely packed lines known as phalanxes. In battle, enemy phalanxes tried to smash through each other's line.

MAKE A SHIELD

You'll need some stiff card, a plastic bucket, scissors, poster paints, glue and sticky tape.

1 Draw round the top of the bucket on to the card. Cut the shape out.
2 Paint a picture on the card, or cut a photograph of a fierce animal from a magazine and stick it on.

3 Cut a handle out of spare card (30 cm by 5 cm). Bend the ends as shown above, then glue and tape them to the shield back.

Ships and the sea

Travelling by ship was far quicker than scaling mountains, so long journeys were usually made by sea. Cargoes of oil, wheat and wine were carried in tubby merchant ships. But merchant ships sailed slowly and were easily captured by pirates.

Fast Athenian warships were built to protect traders. Fleets of these long narrow vessels patrolled the eastern Mediterranean. Out at sea, they cruised under sail. Coming into harbour, or in an attack, they were rowed. A ram at the front was used to sink enemies.

Athens

The largest and most splendid of the Greek city-states was Athens. It is the capital of Greece today, and many of its ancient buildings are still standing.

The city was named after its patron goddess, Athena. It grew up round an acropolis. This was once a hill-top fort, but later it became a holy place with beautiful temples, such as the Parthenon. You can see the acropolis hill at the top of the picture.

KEY TO ATHENS

① Parthenon, the main temple of the goddess Athena
② Statue of Athena
③ Gateway to the acropolis
④ Temple of Athena Victorious
⑤ Agora, the market place

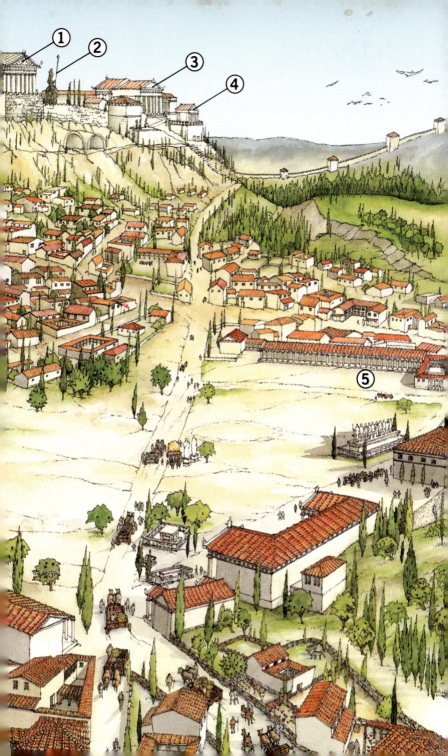

Make a temple

The Parthenon temple was built 2,500 years ago for Athena, the goddess of war and wisdom.

You'll need a sheet of tracing paper, a ruler and a pencil, some thin card, felt-tip pens or crayons, a pair of scissors and some glue.

1 Copy this plan on to the tracing paper, then make it bigger using a photocopying machine.
2 Stick the copy on card and cut around the solid black lines.

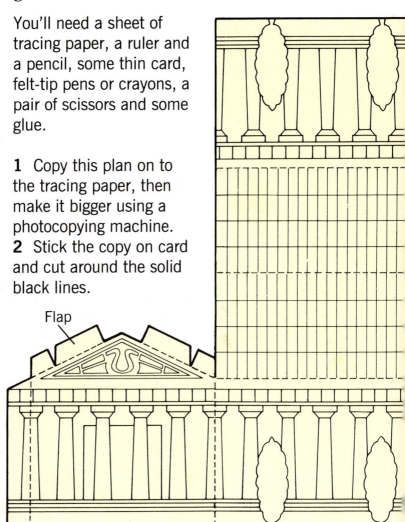

Flap

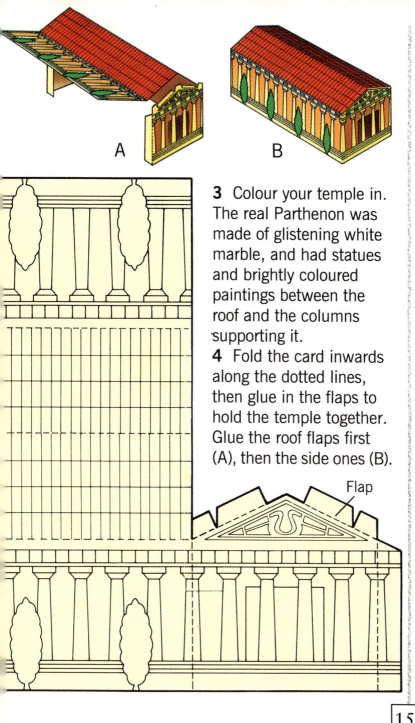

A

B

3 Colour your temple in. The real Parthenon was made of glistening white marble, and had statues and brightly coloured paintings between the roof and the columns supporting it.

4 Fold the card inwards along the dotted lines, then glue in the flaps to hold the temple together. Glue the roof flaps first (A), then the side ones (B).

Flap

Living in a town

There was no roar of traffic in the middle of a Greek town. All the noise came from people and animals.

Narrow streets bustled with people from dawn to dusk. Since towns were built on hills, the streets were often quite steep. They were lined with shops and houses, which were built from mud-bricks and then white-washed.

People shopped with gold or silver coins, like this 4-drachma piece. Each city made its own coins and put a symbol on them. Athenian coins were stamped with an owl, the sign of the goddess Athena.

GOING SHOPPING

Women ran the household and looked after the money, but shopping was usually men's work. Instead of using a purse, they often carried small coins in their mouths.

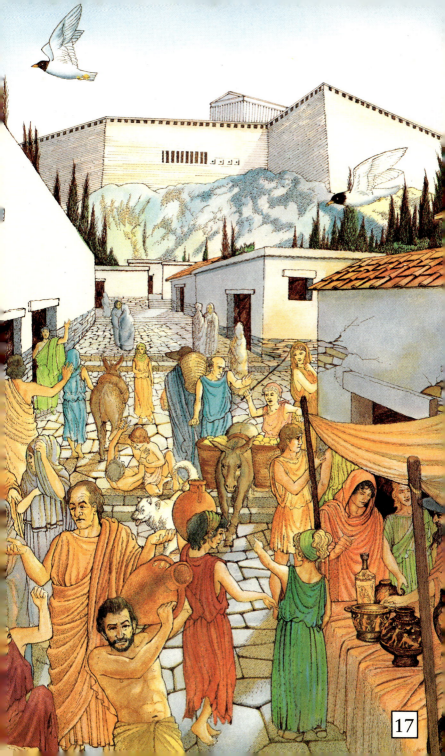

17

Inside a home

Houses were usually built around an open courtyard. In the middle was an altar, where the family prayed.

Women and men had separate living rooms, and never ate together if there were guests. The meals were cooked by wives and daughters or, in wealthy homes, female servants. The men of the house lay on couches, eating from a low table.

KEY TO HOUSE

① Entrance to the house
② Food was stored in sacks and pots
③ Women's room, for cloth-making
④ Bedroom, with low wooden beds
⑤ The men's sitting room
⑥ Bathroom
⑦ Kitchen, with charcoal cooking fire
⑧ Men had their own dining room
⑨ Sometimes a room was let as a shop

As well as cooking all the meals, women were kept busy spinning and weaving cloth, and making clothes for the family. There were no cupboards to put the clothes in – they were stored in wooden chests.

Going to school

Only the sons of freemen went to school in Ancient Greece. Girls were taught by their mothers. Lessons had to be paid for, so boys from poor families probably left school early.

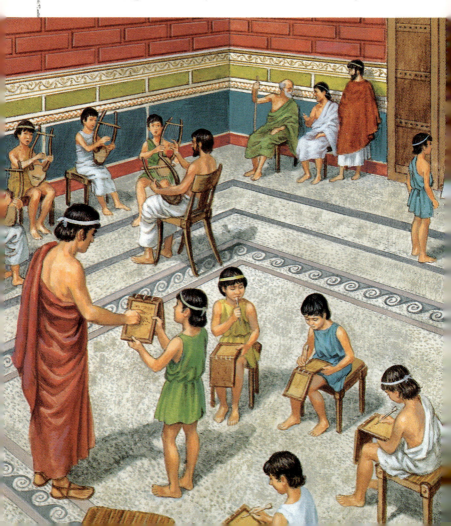

Starting when they were six or seven, boys were taught to read, write, dance and play music. Lots of time was also spent doing athletics.

Children wrote by scratching with a stick called a stylus into a wax tablet. Mistakes were easily rubbed out!

HOME WORK

Girls were taught weaving, and all the other skills they needed to run a household, by their mothers.

At the theatre

The Greeks were the first people to build theatres. Their plays grew out of songs and dances performed for Dionysos, the god of wine. The actors were all men, wearing masks painted to show the character they were playing.

MAKE A GREEK MASK

You'll need a sheet of thin card, some scissors, felt-tip pens, glue and sticky tape, a stick and some thick knitting wool.

1 Draw a face shape with two big eye holes on to the card. Cut around it, and inside the eye holes.

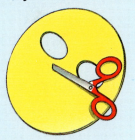

2 Paint a sad face with the mouth turned down on one side of the card, and a happy smiling face on the other side.

3 Glue and tape the stick firmly below the mouth, as a handle.
4 Paint glue around the bottom of the sad mask, then stick on wool to make a beard. When it's dry, turn the mask round and do the same with the happy side.

Storytelling

People in Greece loved listening to stories about their gods and heroes. Even today we still enjoy tales from two great Ancient Greek poems, the *Iliad* and the *Odyssey*. The poems describe the war between the Greeks and the city of Troy, as well as the victorious Greek warriors' long journey home, and all their amazing adventures.

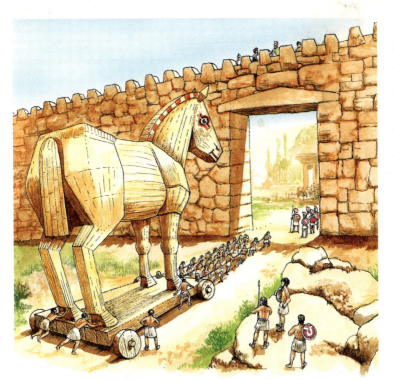

The *Iliad* and *Odyssey* tell us much about Greek legends and history. The Trojan War is said to have ended after the people of Troy were tricked into letting enemy soldiers hiding inside a wooden horse into their city.

People used to think both poems were written by one man, Homer. It is more likely that over hundreds of years, many poets told and retold the stories.

Greek gods

The Greeks believed in a big family of gods and goddesses. The heads of the whole family were the king and queen of the gods, Zeus and his wife Hera. They lived with all the other gods in a land above the clouds over Mount Olympus, the highest mountain peak in Greece.

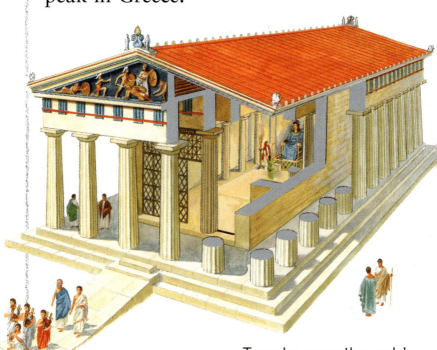

Temples were the gods' homes. There was often a statue of the god inside.

WHO AM I?

Each god or goddess controlled different things on Earth – from the seas and oceans, to music and poetry. Some of their names and jobs are listed below. Can you match the gods and goddesses with their pictures? (The answers are on page 30.)

① **Athena**
Goddess of war and wisdom

② **Ares**
God of war

③ **Aphrodite**
Goddess of love and beauty

④ **Poseidon**
God of the sea

⑤ **Zeus**
King of the gods

⑥ **Demeter**
Goddess of farming and the harvest

⑦ **Artemis**
Goddess of hunting

⑧ **Apollo**
God of music

Olympic Games

The very first Olympic Games were held nearly 2,800 years ago, as part of a festival for Zeus. They took place at a town called Olympia, where there was a special temple for the god.

The Games lasted for five days, and they were held every four years. All of the athletes were men. Women could take part in separate games during a festival for the goddess Hera.

Male athletes didn't wear any clothes – one reason why women couldn't take part in the same games as them. This man is about to throw a discus. You can still watch discus-throwers at athletics meetings today. The first modern Olympic Games were held in 1896.

HOST YOUR OWN OLYMPICS

Try holding your own games at school or in the local park. You'll need lots of space, a long tape measure, and a piece of chalk to mark starting and finishing lines, and distances jumped or thrown.

1 Hundred-metre-dash
Compare your time with the world record – ask for help in the library to look this up in a book.

2 Long jump
Greek athletes used to carry a weight in each hand. Try making your jump without a weight, then do it carrying something in each hand!

3 Discus throwing
Make sure there aren't any windows nearby. Throw a plastic plate or a frisbee.

The winning Greek athlete was given a crown of leaves. Make your own by cutting leaf-shapes from green paper, and stapling them to a head-sized piece of knotted elastic.

Glossary

amphitheatre – a large, circular building where gladiator fights and other entertainments were put on

aqueduct – a bridge-like channel that carried water

atrium – the hall of a house

baths – where the Romans went to wash, exercise, meet with friends and relax

circus – a large, oval building where chariot races took place

empire – a large area of land ruled by an emperor

forum – a market place or open space, where people held meetings

freeman – someone who is a citizen of a state and not a slave

gladiator – a man trained to fight with other gladiators or with wild animals

legionary – a Roman soldier

mosaic – a pattern made with tiny tiles or stones

peristyle – a walled garden

slave – a person who belongs to someone else, who must do everything their owner says

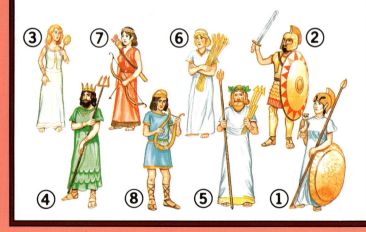